D1245287

The Photography of Paul Briol: A Centennial Tribute

The Cincinnati Historical Society
Cincinnati, Ohio, 1989

Gale E. Peterson
Director

Dottie L. Lewis
Editor

Robin Lippelman
Assistant Editor

Eberhard + Eberhard
Design

Cincinnati Milacron Media Services
Typesetting

Hennegan Company
Printing

The Cincinnati Historical Society gratefully acknowledges the financial support of The Louise Taft Semple Foundation and The Hennegan Company for the processing and cataloging of the Paul Briol Photograph Collection and the publication of this centennial tribute.

2

Paul Briol with incredible
energy and imagination photographed the people and
buildings of Cincinnati, the
city he loved; the unpredicta-
ble Ohio River, and the fields
and forests of the surrounding
region.

What a Father!

Jan Briol Chinnock McLean

To a small girl growing up in College Hill, Paul Briol was an unusual, loving, and exciting father. When reading me a bedtime story, he made up whole sections and endings of the stories. My constant refrain was a partly enchanted, partly exasperated, "Read what it says!" But he never did and it became a joke and a bond between us.

This mixed feeling of delight and frustration characterized our relationship for many years.

In about 1915 Mary Elizabeth Emerson met Paul Briol at Grace Episcopal Church in College Hill where he was attempting to extricate himself from a quickly lamented offer to teach Sunday school.

This rather short, wiry, and attractive volcano of creative activity bowled her over. His sandy hair and mustache were curly and rather bushy. His hazel eyes behind steel rimmed glasses were lively and curious. He wore a beret and smoked a pipe at a jaunty angle. His open, informal manner was colored by his European background. His talent for relationships and his sex appeal must have been apparent then. He lived with his Swiss born parents and sister, Almeé, in the Glenwood Apartments. His father, a Presbyterian minister, and his mother and sister, both artists, were partially dependent on his income as photographer and a columnist for the *Enquirer*. His columns under the title of "Old World Chitchat," using his pseudonym, M. Coligny, appeared regularly for several years during and after World War I. These columns and the pressure of photographing news events kept him going full steam. He had no car and often lugged his bulky 8 x 10" view camera and tripod on streetcars all over town. He was an exciting breath of fresh air to Mary's rather confined conventional life.

Mother had grown up in a comfortable upper-middle class home, surrounded by family in the "big house" next door at the corner of Larch and Belmont avenues. Cushioned by household help, she had pursued her education from Miss Ely's Preparatory School to graduation at Wellesley College. She had an active and intellectually curious mind with a deep love of nature and spiritual awareness. Her thought processes tended to be logical and consistent, though her health had been rather frail during her early adult years with a lingering suspicion of tuberculosis.

I have followed the development of their relationship through a collection of letters from their first tentative notes through the impassioned daily letters when she spent months in a tuberculosis sanitarium in Minnesota, to his three months in New Haven in 1921, where he learned the book business, and those to me when I was married and living in Germany and New York. The richness of their spiritual and deeply caring relationship spills from the bundle of yellowed pages, which she tied with red ribbons. The story is all there. The spiritual and physical dependency, gradually being eroded by Paul's need for independence and pursuit of his own interests, his impatience with himself and others, his growing need for relationships with other women, to his gradual decline following his automobile accident in 1950.

They married in 1920, lost a son at birth in 1921 and welcomed me in 1923. Initially I was named Joan after Jeanne d'Arc, but I could not pronounce that and it soon became Jan.

My early years were brightened by his nightly arrival home. We always knew when he was coming because he blew the steamboat whistle on the old Pontiac a block or so away on Belmont Avenue. By the time he roared up the driveway at 1812 Larch Avenue, my mother and I were on the steps to greet him.

At that time he was manager of The Book Shelf, a unique store in the Doctors Building on Garfield Place. Its long, narrow length was lined with floor-to-ceiling shelves of books, with tables down the center strewn with more books. At the end of the room were tables and easy chairs surrounding a glowing fireplace. The Children's Corner was there, complete with small chairs for easy browsing. Browsing was encouraged with the feeling that one might spend the day reading and never be pressured to purchase a book. The only pressure came from my father who frequently sent someone he liked or disliked a book he felt "they ought to read!" — and those he disliked received a bill.

One night Paul was working late and went out alone with the week's deposits to drive the few blocks to the bank. In the alley he was accosted by a robber who tried to get the car and money away from him. He valiantly held on the steering wheel while the man beat him on the head with a hammer. He lost the money but not the car.

The Book Shelf also featured gala literary dinners for the city's reading elite. With dinner tables and

Jan Briol Chinnock McLean lives in Westport, Connecticut, where she is an artist-in-residence doing painting and sculpting at the Westport Arts Center.

chairs set up down the center aisle prominent literary lions of the day addressed the group on a wide variety of topics. These were followed by lively question-and-answer sessions.

During this period my father and his close friend Howard Henderson, a remarkable and talented man, traversed the hills and valleys and steeples of the city, documenting many now famous vistas. The result was *City of Rivers and Hills*, published in 1925 which, it was said, "revealed Cincinnati to herself."

As the depression grew in 1930 there came dark rumblings from the board which governed the affairs of the store. The store's location and lack of aggressive selling policy threatened its closure. My father ranted and raved against "Mr. Conservative," Robert A. Taft, the member of the board whom he considered the most threatening. Sadly, business interests prevailed. The store's doors, with the ships' lanterns on either side, closed for good in 1930.

This was a dark time at 1812 Larch Avenue, the comfortable home that had been in my mother's family for years. Mother had studied pre-school education when I was nursery school age. She opened a small nursery school in the front bedroom of our house. Little tables, chairs, books, and toys took over. She recruited her charges, often by walking door to door, finally ending up with eight pre-schoolers who came mornings five days a week. When I came home from

school at noon, I experienced my first sense of sibling rivalry. As an only child, I had had my mother's total attention and devotion. Now there were strangers in the house.

There was little money and constant worry those early years as my father attempted to build a photography business based on "photographs that are pictures." Not previously a portrait photographer, he had to become one. His honesty would never let him use the tricks of the trade to glamorize a face or erase warts and wrinkles. His exasperation with some vain sitters was legendary. His eye for the beauty in nature has seldom been equalled. His eye for character versus surface beauty in portraiture was often appreciated more by men than women, including me. In college, when I was unable to get him to take the glamour photo of me I desired, I went to the top "glamourizer" in town and sent Paul the bill. I don't think he ever quite understood — or forgave me.

As his reputation grew, his work took more and more time away from family. My first memory of eating in a restaurant was one Thanksgiving with my mother while my father photographed someone else's family feast.

Christmas during those years was spare for us. The disappointment of a second hand bike, hand me downs that didn't fit and the near crisis of a "no tree Christmas." This was saved on Christmas Eve by the kindness of our neighbors,

By the mid-1920's the Book Shelf under Briol's management was a center of local culture and literary discussion. It was located at 112 Garfield Place in the former home of the Seasongood family.

While managing the Book
Shelf Briol photographed
many Cincinnati scenes
which he used in his book,
The City of Rivers and Hills,
published in 1925 by the Book
Shelf.

Frank and Pierson Davis' parents. But the special glow of carefully lit candles on the tree presided over by Grandmere, Paul's mother, was the highlight of each season.

As the depression continued, my mother's nursery school dwindled. All this time, indeed since I was two years old, Mary Thomas, a remarkable black woman from Georgia, kept the household moving, working as maid, cook, babysitter, and companion. Instead of letting Mary Thomas go, and attempting to do work for which she was ill prepared, Mother took a job with the WPA federal writers project. She found doing research into Ohio's history and her contact with the writers highly stimulating.

During the 1930's Paul was a devoted father who took me along on assignments on the Ohio River boats, in rural Kentucky, and elsewhere. When Mary first met Paul, he had a tent in the woods behind the Ohio Military Institute in College Hill. His need to escape daily frustrations led to his acquisition of a small cottage on the Little Miami River. In time this was sold and he bought a Japanese style cottage from Dr. Tashiro, a distinguished scholar at the University of Cincinnati. "The camp" straddled a steep hill on stilts. Its screened-in front porch was built with a tatami mat platform. Sleeping there, with its unique smells, country sounds, morning mists over the river, and trees dripping with dew were special times. My childhood friend and next door neighbor, Pierson Davis, often went along. We remember stopping at Foster's General Store, before the high viaduct went over it, to buy a fifty pound block of ice and other supplies. We thought it wonderful to have Carnation condensed milk on our cereal. We cherish our memories of the drives home at night over Sleepy Hollow Road when Paul turned out the car light and made all sorts of ghost like and scary noises to give us a jolly good fright.

We also were used as models on some of Paul's assignments. Pierson appeared as a news boy and I as an orphan.

During those years my parents had an active social life with several other couples on College Hill. They loved to dress in formal attire — that is everyone but Paul who squawked loudly about having to be squeezed into a "monkey suit." The couples traipsed from house to house, eating a different course at each one until they reached the dessert house where they concluded the evening with hilarious games of charades. I was watching one night through the stair railing as they strung my father, dressed as cupid in a diaper, upon a rope attached to a hook in a doorway. The rope broke and he crashed in a sudden descent, to everyone's vast amusement.

About 1936 my great aunt, Sarah Simpson, died. Mother was included in her will, but more important to me was the fact that we were given our first radio. My father called it "the talking machine" and from then on newscasts blasted at us as we ate dinner. But I loved it because I could now listen at home to "Tom Mix" and "Inner Sanctum."

We had always had a large console Victrola in the library, that wonderful book stuffed room with a fireplace of Shakespeare character tiles. My father loved to play classical music as loud as possible while waving his arms and body about as conductor.

The dining room featured a large picture window, topped by an arched Tiffany glass of graceful grapes and leaves. It looked out on the garden and beyond to the pasture. Until the pasture was sold we had a barnyard full of chickens, a cow for milk, and a black faced sheep my father gave me one Easter. His excitement and sheer joy sometimes led to his shooting off firecrackers in the dining room fireplace as friends were gathered around the expanded table. I remember those meals as lively and animated by teasing and good stories, loud bangs, and lots of smoke.

A neighbor and friend of Jan Briol's, Pierson Davis, appeared as a newsboy in one of her father's photographs.

In the spring of 1937, my mother achieved a long held dream — to go to Japan and visit her sister and brother-in-law, Ruth and Howard Hannaford and their son Hugh. They were Presbyterian missionaries who had been teaching in Tokyo for years. I was excused from classes at University School in April to pursue an experimental type of education. After three months in Japan, we visited China, and then, on the Trans-Siberian Railroad across the Soviet Union to Moscow. We continued through Poland, Hungary, and much of Europe except Germany, where the Nazis held siege.

My father had not joined us because he felt that being away so long would destroy his hard-won position as one of Cincinnati's most sought after photographers. Always fluent in French, he had by this time become acquainted with many in the foreign and emigré community. Camp, with its open Sunday afternoon gatherings, was becoming the social center of his life. Mother, who had suffered throughout the long separation, quickly became part of this pattern. You never knew who would be there, friends brought friends; there were people from the University, the Symphony, the Charter Party, and everywhere in between. Paul always cooked a great pot of "soup" in the pressure cooker — which on at least one occasion blew up and left an incredible array of vegetables, spices, bay leaves, and meat all over the raftered ceiling. People talked, argued, laughed, climbed up on the roof to drink and enjoy the air, took long walks up creeks and over fields. The potbellied stove glowed through its Eisenglass eye; the orange peels on top let off their aroma, often joined by burning incense. The record player vibrated with all sorts of music from classical to ethnic dances. Some of the best times were had in wild, abandoned dancing. During the long years of World War II the haunting voice of Edith Piaf and the stirring Marseillaise brought strong emotional responses.

The annual New Year's Eve Party became a legendary event. Paul insisted on everyone wearing a costume. His was always outrageous. He once came as the Pope in red robes and a corkscrew cross dispensing "heavy water." These parties ended after much singing and dancing, with a "loving cup," containing a lethal combination of liquors, whiskey, and wine, passed round the circle.

During the war, Paul was busier than ever. He did a great deal of work at Wright Field and other defense installations. He continued doing weddings, as well as portraits, often of young people in the armed forces. Many of the prominent personalities who came for sittings enjoyed the ambiance of the Bohemian studio and the glass of brandy proffered to put them at ease. Sir Eugene Goosins and Elizabeth Schwartzkopf, the opera diva, were among the more famous.

After the war, for the first time in his life, he had savings in the bank. He had never been one to save, or manage money well, always preferring to buy satin when cotton would do. In true Paul Briol style, he took off in his blue Hudson with American flag lashed to the side for the national parks of the West. He returned, broke, but with a wealth of new work. Mary's involvement in the Charter Party, the Woman's City Club, and social causes kept her particularly active during this time.

Paul returned to his studio on Eighth Street opposite Garfield Park and continued documenting the expanding Cincinnati.

By this time, I had graduated from the University of Cincinnati and the Philadelphia School of Occupational Therapy and was working in Boston. These were rather lonely years for my mother, so she was delighted when I returned in 1949 with my husband Frank Chinnock to enable him to complete a master's degree at the Cincinnati Conservatory of Music. We lived at home. It was not easy. My father, always a man impatient with himself and others in the family, had in time become even more so. His patience in "waiting for the light" in photography did not apply to family relationships.

After some years of total devotion to my mother, his attraction to women led him into long-term involvements. He was stimulated by interesting minds and capable single women who were free to accompany him on picture taking trips and other jaunts.

This was very difficult for my mother, but her gratitude in having him, and her incredible tolerance for the behavior of others earned her the name "Saint" from her many friends.

Whatever happened throughout their forty some years together, his respect and love were steadfast. She was the anchor to which he always returned.

In June 1950, while returning from camp with a friend his car was hit broadside by a Greyhound bus. A friend of the family's happened upon the accident before the ambulance arrived. She assumed him dead and crossed his arms over his chest. He was so badly injured that she did not recognize him. He spent a week in a semi-coma as a result of head injuries and then began the long mending process.

He was never the same again. His fiery spirit was gone. In its place was a more benign quiet. His long-term memory remained quite good but everyday events were sometimes hazy. His life long controlled drinking now became a problem.

In time Paul and Mary were no longer able to manage the large house on Larch Avenue, so in 1962, we finally convinced them to move east to live with me and my husband and three young boys.

At that time the old carriage house was full of Paul's negatives and thousands of prints. (He had had to give up his Eighth Street studio). They were piled helter skelter, uncategorized, usually unlabeled and unsigned. (Some, however, were mounted and signed and dated in his trademark, Chinese!). We arranged with Alice Hook, Librarian of the Cincinnati Historical Society, for it to take and maintain the negatives. But the prints, after the family had taken those they wanted, were left to be sold at auction, along with the remaining contents of the house. I had taken boxes of prints but I didn't know how to dispose properly of the rest in that stressful, sad time.

My friend Jane Lotspeich (Mrs. Edgar) came to the rescue. As the auction proceeded all day, she realized that the prints would have to be sold in large lots. She spoke to my aunt and uncle, Ruth and Howard Hannaford who were overseeing the event. They and the auctioneer agreed to remove the prints from the sale. For a nominal fee, Jane acquired over 10,000 unsorted, dusty, often dirty prints — with no idea of what to do with them. After months of

searching she found Pat Brand, Jr., President of the Professional Photographers Association of Greater Cincinnati, whose members agreed to clean them up, mount and hang them for a show of 300 prints at the University of Cincinnati in May 1963. The exhibit was a great success and overwhelming for me to see so many of my father's photographs gathered in one room. Paul felt unable to attend, but Mary, frail but ever loyal, made the flight with me from New York, and proudly enjoyed this tribute so long overdue.

His years in our home in Katonah, New York, with my family were quiet ones. He enjoyed a ground floor back bedroom, with his old bed made from tree trunks which he and his father had felled years before. They had fashioned them into a glorious, gold painted four-poster bed. His last years were spent in a nursing home where he was able to enjoy my newly adopted Vietnamese daughter sitting on his lap. Our last conversations were some of the most rewarding. He died quietly the day before my birthday in August 1969, a little over a year after Mary died.

My family legacy is rich. As an artist and non-professional photographer, I continue to feel Paul's critical eye, "sense of light", and, devotion to craftsmanship. My mother's love of nature nurtured my interest and visual perception.

Paul Briol was not a conventional man! His was not a conventional marriage. He needed freedom to travel, to hike, and explore without constraints. The urge to create his "own space" was constant.

As a child, I adored his inventiveness. As an adolescent, I yearned for a more conventional father who would be "there for me" more often. But now as an adult I understand more of the complexities, needs, and drives of a deeply committed and creative human being.

Briol frequently opened his home to stray animals. A particular favorite was a dog called Mickey. (Photo courtesy Jan Briol McLean)

Views From the Life of Paul Briol: Cincinnati's Unconventional Photographer

Kriste Lindenmeyer

It is Paul Briol's enduring merit . . . .that he has revealed Cincinnati to itself. He has approached his task with the spirit of an artist; he has known how to estimate values. With no eye for the trivial or ephemeral, he has seized upon every aspect of our city which gives it charm and individuality.[1]

Paul Briol's photographs clearly reveal his love of Cincinnati and its surrounding countryside. They also expose the soul of a sensitive human being. Briol was as unorthodox in his art as in his lifestyle. His artistic eye, love of languages and music, intolerance of tyranny and prejudice, fiery determinism, and evangelical spirit made him a complex, interesting, and loved man.

French-Swiss immigrants, Fannie Nusbaum and Pierre Phillippe Briol, married in Greenbay, Wisconsin, on June 6, 1888. A little over one year later, on September 18, 1889, in Spencer, Massachusetts, their first and only son, Paul Auguste Briol was born. Briol's mother was an artist, teacher, and musician.[2] His father was a teacher, scholar, and ordained Presbyterian minister who spoke seven languages.[3] Briol's only sibling was a younger sister named Almeé Fannie Virginia, born in Carthage, Missouri, on June 22, 1893.[4]

Briol's father's occupation as a minister forced the family to relocate frequently. Other than in Massachusetts and Missouri the Reverend Briol served congregations in Argyle and Red Lake Falls, Minnesota; and Gary, South Dakota. In 1903 when Paul Briol was fourteen, the family moved to New Orleans. There the Reverend Briol acted as a Presbyterian missionary and in 1905 founded the First French Presbyterian Church of New Orleans. But, becoming pastor of this tiny congregation of seventeen did not end the Briols' nomadic lifestyle. While in New Orleans they lived at five separate addresses, and Fannie Briol taught music to supplement their income.[5]

The fact that Briol's father was a Presbyterian minister in heavily Catholic New Orleans must have complicated his adjustment to the family's frequent moves.

Friends remember that Briol's father's Protestant evangelism was not generally well accepted by Catholics.[6] Additionally, young Briol's northern accent encouraged his southern classmates to ask him, "Are you a damned Yankee?" But, despite these tauntings, Paul Briol graduated from high school in 1908 and soon moved to St. Louis where he got his first job as a newspaper journalist. It is not clear why Briol left New Orleans so soon after high school graduation,

Kriste Lindenmeyer is a doctoral student in American history at the University of Cincinnati.

His columns "Old World Chit Chat" which he wrote from 1912 to 1920 provide insights to Paul Briol's beliefs as a young man. (Photo courtesy Jan Briol McLean)

nevertheless, it is likely that his parents encouraged him to choose St. Louis because he could live there with his uncle, the Reverend Charles Nusbaum.[7]

But, Briol's stay in St. Louis was relatively brief. In 1909 he moved to Cincinnati where his Uncle Charles arranged for him to live at the home of the Reverend Louis G. Hoeck, minister of the city's Swedenborgian Church.[8] In Cincinnati Briol joined the staff of the Cincinnati *Commercial Tribune* as a journalist and photographer.[9] One of his earliest assignments was to photograph the first rehearsal of the Cincinnati Symphony Orchestra under the leadership of its new conductor Maestro Leopold Stokowski.[10] This was a difficult task due to the poor lighting available in Music Hall and the fact that Briol had no flash equipment.[11] However, he convinced another photographer to share his flash and the resulting picture appeared on the front page of the next day's *Commmercial Tribune* crediting Briol and listing him as an official staff photographer.[12] This classic photograph was Paul Briol's first professionally credited work.

To date no clear records showing how or where Briol learned the art of photography have been found. However, the fact that photojournalism was still a relatively novel phenomenon probably provided him the freedom he needed to develop his skills. The difficulty of transporting photographs speedily over long distances and the cumbersome size of box cameras encouraged few early twentieth century editors to utilize photojournalism extensively.

Although it had been possible to reproduce photographs in newspapers since the Civil War era, early twentieth century news photography was generally limited to portrait style reproductions.[13] This fact coupled with Paul Briol's love of literature and writing encouraged him to continue pursuing his journalistic interests at the same time he was improving his photographic skills.

In 1910 Briol received a greater opportunity to continue this professional path when he left the *Commercial Tribune* and joined the staff of the *Cincinnati Enquirer*.[14] In this new job, Briol was a staff photographer and beginning in May 1912 the author of the paper's "Old-World Chitchat" column.[15] Similar to many other journalists of the period, Briol chose to write under a pseudonym. Interestingly, his choice of "M. Coligny" most likely had special meaning for the son of a French-Swiss Protestant minister.[16]

Briol's "Old-World Chitchat" columns ran regularly Monday through Saturday from May 28, 1912, through November 1, 1920. They cover a broad range of subjects and provide an important insight to Paul Briol's beliefs as a young man. His choice of topics and editorial comments show his intelligence, curiosity, strong belief in Christianity and its traditions, intolerance of tyranny, and above all his evangelical spirit.

One of Briol's favorite topics concerned women and what he perceived as their proper role in society. In many ways he appears to have appreciated intelligent

His photograph of the first rehearsal of Leopold Stokowski conducting the Cincinnati Symphony Orchestra was Briol's first picture published in the *Commercial Tribune*.

women and acknowledged their expanding roles outside of the domestic sphere. Nevertheless, he also showed little tolerance for women who employed radical methods to gain equal rights or "shirked" what he believed to be their maternal "responsibilities."

Several articles laud the accomplishments and independent thinking of some individual women. In one such example Briol praised a British headmistress who was willing to withstand the controversy concerning her teaching of "the mystery of birth" to her female students. In another, Briol admired Maria Montessori and her "system of education that promises to revolutionize ordinary methods of pedagogy." He was especially impressed with the fact that Montessori was the first woman graduate of the University of Rome's medical school. During one column he argued that "the old idea that women should be protected from danger of every kind must soon rapidly die out for the younger generation with its high spirits and its well-balanced nerves will have no traffic with timidity of any sort."[17] These examples seem to suggest his acceptance of women as equals.

But on the other hand, in other articles Paul Briol demonstrated his reluctance to support nontraditional roles for women. Briol condemned British women's rights advocates for their "meddling . . . resumption of suffragette activities." Further, Briol scolded the British government for employing "comedy methods in dealing with these silly and wicked women."[18] Another problem faced by the British in this era was the overwhelming disproportion of women to men in England as a result of the high number of British males killed during the war. Briol warned that "the social effects of sex disproportion are evident in the crumbling of many old ethical standards . . . and [lowered] morality." He held women responsible for maintaining high morals. In such circumstances Briol suggested that married men might be tempted by single women to seek "relations" outside of marriage. Accordingly, argued Briol, the desire of many married women to have fewer children contributed to these difficulties.[19] He loved the company of intelligent women and many were very attracted to him, but, as these examples illustrate, he held some very ambivalent feelings concerning women. Some of his ideas were likely a product of his Christian background and others reflected significant trends of the period.[20]

Another set of issues discussed in Briol's columns were the circumstances of many individuals in Europe during and after World War I. In 1915 he wrote two very sensitive articles describing the plight of French and British soldiers blinded in battle. Another called for the public to extend special caring and tolerance to the "hundreds of 'war

babies' about to be born to unmarried mothers in England."[21] These are only a sample of the many articles written by Briol to describe the sufferings of those in Europe during and after the war.

As the fighting intensified, Briol used his column to inspire support for the countries battling Germany. He praised Britain's Prime Minister David Lloyd George as "an admirable statesman — an active, progressive, frank, full-blooded, horse-sense man." Another column published on May 12, 1917, contended that despite a variety of languages among Allied peoples ("including Japan and the South American republics"), all were striving to preserve civilization and democracy. In other articles Briol expressed appreciation specifically to France.[22] In general his columns held the Allied powers in high esteem.

In contrast with his high esteem for the Allies, Briol wrote very negative articles concerning Germany. One column described Germany's use of poison gas against French soldiers and civilians.

Since Germany set forth on its criminally insane course in the dog days of 1914, *the world has had many painful surprises, but none so terrible as the lesson that the soldier of the spiked helmet spares neither women nor children, and that the doctrine of Military Necessity excuses, nay encourages, any enormity designed to terrorize from deeds of the most unbridled kind to murders of revolting cruelty.*[23]

Another column was illustrated with a drawing of a "homeless, penniless, emaciated" French woman suffering from what Briol described as the German "invasion." Near the end of the war he called for "justice" against Germany — "Give Germany Justice — Nothing More. Her people must reap what they have sown, and they should give a town for a town — a ship for a ship."[24] Briol's support of the Allies and condemnation of Germany during the war was very probably quite well accepted by many of his readers. A strong anti-German feeling existed in the United States during this period, even in a heavily German immigrant area such as Cincinnati.[25]

After the war Briol continued his unrelenting criticism of Germany. Throughout 1919 and 1920 he called for strong punishments against Germany's leadership and its people. Briol contended in a March 4, 1920, article that "as yet we have been able to recognize no sign of regeneration or penitence in the German people."[26] He had little patience for those he viewed as the "criminal aggressors" in the war. However, Briol's friends contend that this criticism was largely political and not necessarily ethnically based.[27]

This viewpoint is particularly evident in his

12

comments on revolutionary events which occurred in Russia during these years. He was sympathetic to the plight of the Russian people and their suffering under the czar. But, Briol denounced the Bolsheviks as "for themselves alone, they subject all others to their exploitation." He contended that the result of Bolshevism is "the foulest, most hateful and sucidal [sic] of all tyrannies." For Briol, Bolshevism was a direct threat to Christianity. He lamented in February 1920 that "the war is not over. We failed to finish it and the Bolsheviks mean to finish us from the Baltic to the Persian Gulf."[28] Briol believed the Bolsheviks, like Germany, were the epitome of evil and anti-Christianity. His hatred of Bolshevism and Germany translated well to the swelling "Red Scare" mentality spreading throughout the United States after the war. His reactions were not unlike those of many other Americans.[29]

Some of Briol's most insightful columns concerned the subject of Asian and American foreign relations. As a high school student in New Orleans, he had met a Chinese scholar who taught him how to write numbers using Chinese characters.[30] Interestingly, Briol used Chinese characters to date and identify his photographs throughout his life. He also had a special fascination for Japanese and Chinese art and furniture. Perhaps these factors influenced him in his *Cincinnati Enquirer* column to condemn "Japanophobia" and encourage better United States Japanese cooperation. In a very prophetic article on January 20, 1920, he warned that the next war might take place in Asia. His column the following day discussed the complicated situation in China during the early twentieth century.[31] While Briol's interpretation of Asian American relations was somewhat limited by his Western viewpoint, his sensitivity and insight into the negative effects fostered by America's racist policies are unusual for the time in which he was writing.[32]

As unceremoniously as he had become the author of "Old-World Chitchat," Briol handed the column over to another journalist in November 1920.[33] His contribution to Cincinnati journalism during this period is generally overshadowed by his photographic artistry. However, it is apparent from his broad range of topics and strongly advocated viewpoints that Briol's journalistic efforts probably influenced the opinions of many readers.

Why Briol left the *Enquirer* in late 1920 is not completely understood. Some have speculated that his anti-German stance may have become an issue of controversy with his editors. Others contend that he might have tired of the pressures associated with a daily column and additional photographic responsibilities. He particularly disliked his assignments to photograph Cincinnati Reds baseball games. Not being a baseball fan made the difficulty of carrying his equipment to the best vantage points in old Crosley Field especially distasteful.[34] Whatever his reasons for leaving the paper were, 1920 was an exciting year for Paul Briol.

The stage for the most outstanding event which occurred in Briol's life in 1920 had actually been set about five years earlier when he met Mary Elizabeth Emerson at Grace Episcopal Church in College Hill, a northern Cincinnati suburb. Mary suffered from symptoms of tuberculosis and sporadically spent time at a sanitarium in Minnesota. Touching love letters exchanged during these periods illustrate Mary and Paul's developing relationship.[35] On May 26, 1920, Mary Emerson and Paul Briol married at the same church in which they had first met.[36]

Born in Cincinnati in 1884, Mary Elizabeth Emerson's background was very different from that of Paul Briol's. She was reared in an upper-middle class home located at the corner of Larch and Belmont avenues in College Hill. As a girl she attended Miss E. Antoinette Ely's Clifton School for Young Ladies and in 1909 graduated from Wellesley College. Following her graduation, she returned to Miss Ely's school as a math teacher.[37] Mary Emerson Briol's parents, Mary Adelpha Simpson and Dudley Emerson, were members of two wealthy and prominent Cincinnati families. Dudley Emerson served as head of the Ohio Military Institute located in College Hill and her mother was active in a number of Cincinnati's philanthropic women's organizations.[38] Her sister, Ruth Emerson Hannaford, was a Presbyterian missionary in Japan. Mary Emerson had two brothers, one of whom, Earl Emerson, headed the Armco Steel Corporation plant in Middletown, Ohio.[39]

Mary Briol possessed the spirit, intelligence, and elegance her new husband found so attractive in women. Likewise, Paul Briol was a debonair young man who emitted a rather European style which Mary Emerson enjoyed very much. In addition, Briol led what looked to Mary Emerson like an exciting lifestyle. He often wore a beret and smoked a pipe. His curly mustache and bushy eyebrows made him uniquely handsome. There was a "spiritual" bond between them that was tied by a shared love of literature, nature, and music. Mary Briol commented in later years that marrying Paul saved her from what she believed might have been a very conventional and dull life.[40]

Upon leaving the *Cincinnati Enquirer* in 1920, Paul Briol began working as manager of what soon became a unique book store in downtown Cincinnati. A board consisting of a variety of influential Cincinnati citizens provided financial backing and business direction for the business venture and sent Briol to New Haven, Connecticut, to learn about the book and publishing business. Excited about the store Briol planned to make it a center for intellectual activity in Cincinnati.[41]

On Monday, May 9, 1921, The Book Shelf opened its doors at 112 Garfield Place. The building was the former elegant home of the Seasongood family. According to an article in the *Cincinnati Tribune*, a reception held on the store's opening day featured the display of "a Bible 250 years old, . . . many rare publications, and 10,000 volumes written by noted authors from all over the world." Its inventory also included over 1,000 children's books and its atmosphere was cozy and warm.

Well chosen colors, tastful [sic] paper, an old fashioned fireplace, agreeable hangings, and, above all, the well-lined cases, produce the recreative literary aspect . . . . The purpose of the store "*was to stimulate the reading of good literature and to supply the wants of Cincinnati book lovers.*"[42]

Indeed, during the early 1920's The Book Shelf was a center of local culture and literary discussion. Special events included dinners featuring guest speakers followed by hotly debated discussions. Sales for the store's third fiscal year

tripled those of its first year of operation. By the mid-twenties The Book Shelf was a popular success. Briol welcomed anyone into his shop and gave away books to people whom he judged could not afford them. He also mailed books to individuals he felt should read them. These unsolicited "gifts" and their accompanying bills were often not welcomed by their recipients.[43]

While managing the store Briol heightened his photographic skills by taking excursions throughout the Cincinnati area with his 8 x 10 inch box camera and tripod. Using some of the picturesque photographs gained on these adventures Briol authored *The City of Rivers and Hills* which The Book Shelf published in 1925.[44] This lovely collection of black and white photographs, dedicated to his wife, Mary, is enhanced by his own artistic descriptions. Its pages have beautifully frozen many aspects of Cincinnati in the 1920's.

But despite the bookstore's early success, Briol's lack of business expertise and the disastrous economic effects of the Great Depression forced The Book Shelf into bankruptcy in 1930.[45] At that time Robert A. Taft, who often disgusted Briol with his "conservative" business as well as political viewpoints, was the company's president. It is difficult to imagine a more unlikely pair of business partners.[46]

During his years at The Book Shelf Paul and Mary Briol set-up housekeeping at their home on 1812 Larch Avenue in College Hill. The house was located on property owned by Mary's maternal grandparents. Next door, in "the big house" lived Mary's parents and maternal grandmother. Early in their marriage, Mary gave birth to a son who was stillborn. The Briol's were heartbroken over this loss. But, they were exuberant when their only child, Joan "Jan" Briol was born in 1923. The twenties were happy years in which they started a family and cultivated an active social life.[47]

After the closing of The Book Shelf, Briol continued his photographic work and opened a studio on the eighth floor of the Doctors' Building located at 19 Garfield Place. There were forty-nine photographic studios listed in the Cincinnati *City Directory* during the early 1930's. Briol's prospective income as a photographer among this heavy competition was especially meager during these trying economic times. But, it was also during this period that Briol began to gain significant recognition as a free lance photographer. Some of his pictures were used as illustrations in two books authored during these years. Captain Frederick Way, Jr. published the first in 1933 and Clark B. Firestone the second in 1936.[48]

During the 1930's Briol gained a reputation as a portrait photographer by taking pictures of some of

Mary Elizabeth Emerson married Paul Briol on May 26, 1920. (Photo courtesy Jan Briol McLean)

Cincinnati's most prominent families.[49] This kind of work helped to pay the bills, but it also took Briol away from his family on holidays so that he might photograph a client's family gathering. In addition, Briol complained that people who had their portraits taken did not really want to see what they actually looked like. One method he utilized to relax his subjects was to engage them in friendly conversation accompanied by a drink before he took their photograph.[50] This practice probably also made portrait photography more palatable to Briol.

Some of Paul Briol's most touching photographs were taken during the 1930's. They document the hard times faced by many Cincinnatians during these years. One picture features a destitute looking family standing in front of their beached houseboat beneath the Southern Railway Bridge. Another silhouettes the shadows of male day laborers waiting for work. The sign above them reads, "All men must be clean and tidy — dirty men will not be sent out." Other photographs show pictures of the Cincinnati Children's home.[51] Briol had a soft spot for the underdog, but he realized

In 1923 Mary and Paul Briol became the parents of a daughter Jan.

that he must at times forgo art in order to make a living.

Money was a problem for the Briols just as it was for most other Americans during the Great Depression. But, the Briols were more fortunate than many. They remained in their home on Larch Avenue and Mary Briol attempted to maintain her family's refined lifestyle despite their economic difficulties. First she operated a small nursery school in the house and later worked with the New Deal's Federal Writers' Project. Mary Thomas, a black woman from Georgia who was employed as the family's live-in maid for many years remained with the Briols despite the economic hard times.[52]

Things appear to have improved somewhat for the family by the late 1930's, as in 1937 Mary Briol and her daughter, Jan (toting a Kodak "Brownie" camera), took an extended trip to visit Ruth Hannaford in Japan. Paul Briol did not join them because he feared leaving his business for such a lengthy period of time.[53] In addition, by the mid-thirties Briol had acquired a small cottage on the Little Miami River in Foster, Ohio.[54] He purchased the property from Shiro Tashiro, a Japanese American professor who taught biochemistry at the University of Cincinnati Medical School from 1919 to 1955. For the next fifteen years Briol religiously made weekend retreats to the cottage he lovingly referred to as "Camp."[55]

Briol's property was located on Davis Road, on the banks of the Little Miami River. The cottage was built in a Japanese style and some of its furnishings reflected the Asian ethnicity of its original owner. Because of Briol's interest in Asian culture, the Japanese influence present at the Camp pleased him. A handsome Steinway upright piano stood in one room. Hundreds of photographs adorned the walls, a variety of books lined the shelves, and loud classical, folk, or "jazz" music constantly resounded from the phonograph. Huge national flags of a variety of nations hung inside and outside the cottage. The aroma of orange peels placed on the wood stove competed with that of the "famous" stews Briol concocted for his many guests. During the Camp's existence the inviting atmosphere and Briol's stimulating company drew a constant stream of visitors.

Saturday was "Paul's private day" at the cottage. Only his specially invited guests were allowed to visit on Saturday. Increasingly over the years Briol's "special guest" was likely to be an attractive younger woman with whom he chose to spend his time. Mary Briol suffered over her husband's extramarital affairs, but she tolerated the situation because she believed that he needed "Camp" and its "accompaniments" to keep him happy. She offered to give him a divorce, but Briol refused. In hindsight, it may be difficult

to understand such a relationship. However, Mary Briol's friends and family describe her as one of the most tolerant and patient individuals they have ever known. She accepted people for whom they were, including her husband whom she felt made her life interesting.[56]

Sunday was open house which meant that anyone was welcome. Briol's close friends often brought others with them and the circle widened by word of mouth. Some of the visitors were members of the local emigré community. Briol, who spoke fluent French, was especially attracted to French immigrants and other refugees fleeing Hitler's oppression. Other visitors were members of the local intelligentsia connected with the University of Cincinnati. Some were musicians working with the Cincinnati Symphony Orchestra and Zoo Opera. Reform minded political supporters were another segment of Briol's varied group of guests. Even Mary Briol attended Sundays. Sometimes daughter Jan and nephew David T. Harvey, his sister Almeé's son, also came along.[57]

Besides the phonograph, books, and concerts provided by visitors on the Steinway (many of them

Briol purchased his "Camp" from Shiro Tashiro, a Japanese American professor who taught biochemistry at the University of Cincinnati.

accomplished concert pianists) there was a variety of recreational activities. Summertime brought swimming in the river and sunbathing on the building's tin roof. Dancing and singing were year round entertainments. The highlight of the winter season was a grand costume party held each New Year's Eve. Briol loved to dress as a Catholic Archbishop in flowing robes adorned with a corkscrew pendant in place of the usual gilded cross. In this costume he dispensed "heavy water" to his guests. Drinking accompanied each visit to camp and all sessions ended with a passing of the "loving cup" filled with a potent, but sumptuous, mixture of liquors and wine. It cannot be overstated how much Briol loved his visits to Camp. He tried to travel there each weekend, whatever the weather.[58]

The Briols also attended formal parties and social functions with friends in College Hill, but increasingly the social lives of Paul and Mary Briol separated. Their home on Larch Avenue became known as "Mary's house" and she devoted larger amounts of her attention to her work with the Woman's City Club, the Charter Party, and the League of Women Voters.[59] Nevertheless, daily life in the Briol home during the late 1930's and early 1940's followed a fairly consistent pattern of elegant style, almost Victorian in nature

— except, of course, for a few of Paul and Mary Briol's eccentricities which made things interesting.

The three bedroom Larch Avenue house was furnished with impressive Rookwood Pottery fireplaces, fine oriental rugs, and an extensive library stocked with literary classics, poetry, and books on nature and animals. Correct English, manners, and dress were considered important behavior by the Briols. However, some things about the household made it unique. Briol frequently opened his home to stray animals — despite the fact that many were flea infested and disruptive. One of his favorites was a three legged Spitz dog. Cats were the most numerous house guests and some even went along with him to Camp. For her part, Mary kept a closet full of blue canvas walking shoes with yellow rubber soles as evidence of her travels. David Harvey, Paul Briol's nephew, lived with Paul, Mary, and Jan from the time he was in the fifth grade until he graduated from Hughes High School in 1951 and entered college. Harvey remembers each day began with the same routine. Mary Thomas called the family to breakfast with the chime of a bell. The meal consisted of tea, fruit, warm cereal, egg, bacon, sausage, and toast. Paul Briol regularly interrupted his meal between the fruit and cereal to go outside and warm-up his blue 1939 Hudson which he drove to his downtown office. The car's loud engine would race throughout the morning meal waiting for Briol to leave for work.[60]

Briol enjoyed a booming business during World War II. Earlier in 1938 he moved his office to the second floor of a building at 114 Garfield Place.[61] He increasingly received commissions to photograph the facilities of Cincinnati area corporations and private gardens. During World War II, Briol photographed local defense plants and affiliated businesses. As an added benefit his association with the U.S. Defense Department provided him with a privileged gas rationing status which was especially important to Briol because it allowed him to drive his car regularly to Camp despite gas rationing. Near the end of the war *Look* magazine purchased a few of Briol's pictures to include in their publication *Look at America: The Country You Know and Don't Know* (published in 1946). These professional successes provided Briol with money in the bank for the first time in his life.[62]

So in the spring of 1946 with money in his pocket, Briol climbed into his 1939 Hudson, lashed an American flag to its side, and drove west to Yosemite, California. Mary Briol did not accompany her husband on his adventure. Instead, various friends traveled with him along the way. In Ansel Adams style he took a plethora of photographs

The annual New Year's Eve Party at "Camp" became a legendary event with the guests coming in costume. One year Briol dressed as a Catholic archbishop in long flowing robes dispensing "heavy water" from a corkscrew cross. (Photo courtesy Jan Briol McLean)

For his stationery Briol used
his photograph of three children looking up at the statue
of Lincoln in Lytle Park.

during his journey that greatly broadened his portfolio.[63]

By the late 1940's Briol was clearly the most sought after photographer in Cincinnati. His "signature" was his technique of superimposing magnificent skies on all his photographs of Cincinnati scenes. This method is especially revealing of Briol's artistic style. He continued to use his huge 8 x 10 inch box camera even after more sophisticated equipment was developed. Although he took a number of colored photographs during and after the Second World War, he was never very comfortable with the light meters necessary to use colored film properly. Instead, Briol preferred his "old fashioned" black and white methods with which he felt he could easily emphasize "art" over technology.[64]

In many cases Briol went to great lengths to get just the right vantage point for his photographs. During one particular session, he climbed to the top of the Roebling Suspension Bridge to get the perfect camera shot. While he was standing inside a small enclosure at the top of the bridge's tower, a wind blew the door shut and locked him inside. Fortunately, someone on the ground noticed that he had not come down from his perch and called the police to set him free.[65] On another occasion, he was struck by a passing car when he placed his camera too close to the road in order to get a particular viewpoint of a traffic accident in Covington, Kentucky.[66]

Briol's successful photographic career was tragically interrupted in 1950 when he was seriously injured in a car accident. Briol and a companion, Mrs. Joselyn Farmer, left his Camp in Foster at about three o'clock one afternoon on an excursion to buy a baby gift for a friend.[67] Visibility was poor and road conditions were slippery due to a severe rainstorm. According to newspaper reports, at approximately 3:30 p.m. about one mile south of Mason, Ohio, on Route 42 Briol attempted to pass a truck and hit a Greyhound bus traveling in the opposite direction. Thirty-five passengers on the bus were slightly hurt, but Briol and Farmer received serious head and body injuries.[68]

Paul Briol never fully recovered from this accident. He attempted to keep up his photographic work, but it simply became too difficult and he closed his downtown studio in 1955. His friends and family contend that he was never quite the same after the accident. Probably the most painful aspect for Briol was that he was no longer able to "hold Camp." His drinking became a serious problem rather than a pleasure and his health declined.[69]

In 1962 Briols closed their College Hill home and moved to Katonah, New York, to live with their daughter Jan.[70] The family's household furnishings were sold at auction in May 1962, but over 6,000 of Briol's negatives had been transferred to the Cincinnati Historical Society. The quick

During World War II Briol photographed Wright Aeronautical Corporation, a local defense plant.

thinking of a close family friend, Jane Lotspeich, saved his extensive personal collection of prints from the auctioneer's gavel. She arranged with Mary Briol's family to remove the photographs from the auction so that they might be displayed in an exhibition sometime in the future. From May 1962 to January 1963, Lotspeich tirelessly searched for a way to provide such an exhibition. Ultimately the Cincinnati Professional Photographers' Association agreed to sponsor the event. They would provide their expertise in selecting, mounting, and framing 300 prints for the show and the University of Cincinnati agreed to provide display space in Tangeman Center on the campus.[71]

From May 12 to 26, 1963, the Paul Briol exhibit at the University of Cincinnati drew a wide range of admirers. The Cincinnati *Post-Times Star* reported that "some 50

prominent Cincinnatians are serving on the exhibition committee." The paper quoted Jane Lotspeich as saying that "the remarkable thing . . . is that we have not needed to ask for any money. Even printing [was] donated."[72] At the same time the *Cincinnati Enquirer* ran a four page pictorial of Briol's photographs in its Sunday magazine.[73] Briol was too feeble to attend the exhibition himself, but it was a fitting tribute to a talented and loved Cincinnatian.

Mary Elizabeth Emerson Briol died in February 1968 in Katonah, New York. A memorial service and burial was held at Spring Grove Cemetery in Cincinnati.[74] Paul Auguste Briol died a little over one year later on Sunday, August 3, 1969, in a nursing home near his daughter's home in Katonah. A memorial service and private burial was held at Spring Grove the following Saturday.[75]

After World War II Briol took off with a flag lashed to the side of his blue Hudson to photograph the national parks of the West. He returned with a wealth of new material.

20

His signature was his technique of superimposing magnificent skies on his photographs.

Since Briol's death two tributes to his artistry have been featured in Cincinnati. In 1981 the Cincinnati Historical Society published an appointment calendar and a collection entitled *Paul Briol: Cincinnati 1925-1950* featuring some of his prints.[76] In 1983, an exhibition of Briol's photographs returned to the University of Cincinnati's Tangeman Center.[77]

The spirit of Paul Briol, who modestly called himself a "scenic, portraitural, architectural and industrial" photographer, lives on in his pictures. In an advertisement for his studio Briol wrote, "I hope and believe that the pictures I may make of your home, your gardens, your family, your structural creations or your business may be a delightful surprise."[78] Many would agree that his desire has been fulfilled and that their lives have been enriched for having known him.

1. Henry Wald Bettman, M.D. introduction to *The City of Rivers and Hills*, by Paul Briol (Cincinnati, 1925), p. 2.
2. Fannie Nusbaum Briol was born in Switzerland on May 24, 1857. She immigrated to the United States June 16, 1884. Her father was a tutor at the Court in Vienna, Austria. Her brother, Charles Nusbaum, also taught there, but left his position in a dispute concerning Protestant beliefs. He then joined a French Protestant group which led him to many sights around the world and eventually to the United States. He founded a French colony in Tennessee and served as pastor of the Swedenborgian Church in St. Louis, Missouri. Another brother, Robert Nusbaum, founded a school near Vevey, Switzerland. Telephone interview conducted with David T. Harvey, September 16, 1989; "Aged Minister Expires at Hospital," *Cincinnati Enquirer*, January 26, 1935, p. 14; Howard Henderson, "Notes on the Life of Paul Auguste Briol," essay prepared March 3, 1963, in possession of Jan Briol McLean.
3. Pierre Phillippe Briol (1853-1935) was born in Villy, Switzerland in 1853. As a young man he immigrated to Montreal, Canada to study at McGill University and then attended McCormick Theological Seminary in Chicago, Illinois. He was ordained by the Presbyterian Church in San Francisco, California in 1887. He married Fannie Nusbaum in 1888. The couple had two children, Paul Auguste born in 1889, and Almee Fannie Virginia born in 1893. In 1913 the Reverend Briol was a delegate to the World Sunday School Conference held in Zurich, Switzerland. During 1915-1916 he preached in various churches throughout France in the place of ministers who were serving at the front. Briol came to Cincinnati in 1917. He spent several months during 1918-1919 teaching French to American soldiers at Camp Sheridan in Montgomery, Alabama, as a Young Men's Christian Association (YMCA) educational secretary. In 1920 he began to conduct services in French at the First Presbyterian Church in Walnut Hills. Starting in 1930 he regularly held French services at the Italian Presbyterian Church at Magnolia and Elm streets. During the 1930's he taught a Federal Emergency Relief Administration French language class "because of his great interest in the Administration's work." The Reverend Briol died in Cincinnati in January 1935. *Ibid.*; "Preaches in French in Italian Church," *Cincinnati Enquirer*, January 16, 1930, p. 2.
4. Almee Fannie Virginia Briol was born in Carthage, Missouri June 22, 1893, and died in Cincinnati, Ohio on October 9, 1976. She had one child, David T. Harvey born in Cincinnati October 9, 1933. Harvey interview.
5. Louis Voss, D.D., *Presbyterianism in New Orleans and Adjacent Places*, (New Orleans, 1931), p. 79. *Soards Directory*, (New Orleans) photocopies of pages listing Briol family residences from 1904-1913 from Historic New Orleans Collections, New Orleans, Louisiana.
6. Interview conducted with Kenneth Caster at his home in Cincinnati July 24, 1989.
7. Henderson, "Notes on the Life of Paul Auguste Briol," p. 1.
8. A search of the Cincinnati *City Directory* from 1912-1917 suggests that Briol lived with the Reverend Hoek until his parents and sister Almee moved to Cincinnati in 1917. *Ibid.; Williams City Directory*, vols. 1912-1917 (Cincinnati: Williams Publishing Company).

9. The Cincinnati *Commercial Tribune* was a daily morning newspaper which began publication October 2, 1843, as the *Daily Cincinnati Commercial*. The paper's name was changed to the *Cincinnati Daily Commercial* November 13, 1965. The newspaper merged with the *Cincinnati Gazette* and became the *Commercial Gazette* on January 4, 1883. A merger with the *Tribune* in 1896 resulted in a name change to the *Commerical Tribune* on February 14, 1898. The paper ceased publication on December 3, 1930. For a history of the paper see *Commercial Tribune*, June 17, 1923, p. 3; reference card located at the Cincinnati Historical Society (CHS).
10. Leopold Stokowski served as the conductor of the Cincinnati Symphony Orchestra (CSO) from 1909-1912; a variety of CSO papers are located at CHS.
11. Flash powder was the major source of illumination for photographers until Paul Vierkotter patented the first version of a flash bulb in 1925. In 1929 a more sophisticated version was patented in Germany as the Vacu-Blitz and in the United States as the Photoflash Lamp. With this equipment pictures could virtually be taken anywhere. Beaumont Newhall, *The History of Photography from 1839 to the Present Day*, (New York, 1964), p. 157.

Joselyn Farmer, a College Hill resident and a chemist, was with Briol in his car when he had his serious accident in 1950.

12. *Commercial Tribune*, November 1909, p. 1.

13. Newhall, *The History of Photography From* 1830 *to the Present Day*, pp. 175-177.

14. The *Cincinnati Enquirer* began publication as the *Daily Enquirer* on April 10, 1841. It changed its name to the *Daily Message* on April 27, 1844 and the *Cincinnati Daily Enquirer* on January 21, 1845. The paper became the *Cincinnati Enquirer* beginning February 13, 1872; CHS newspaper reference file.

15. M. Coligny, "Old-World Chitchat" *Cincinnati Enquirer*, May 28, 1912.

16. Gaspar de Coligny (1519-1572) was admiral of France and leader of the Protestant Huguenots during the first half of the Wars of Religion. On August 22, 1572, Coligny was shot and wounded in Paris in an assassination attempt. On August 24 he was attacked and thrown to his death from an open window. His body was mutilated by a Paris mob and hanged on the givet at Montfaucon; *Encyclopaedia Britannica*, 11th ed., s.v. "Gaspard de Coligny," p. 683.

17. Coligny, "Should Girls Be Told the Mystery of Birth?" *Cincinnati Enquirer*, March 2, 1914, p. 6; "Freedom for Self Development is the Keynote of the Montissori [sic] System of Education that Promises to Revolutionize Ordinary Methods of Pedagogy," *Cincinnati Enquirer*, March 4, 1914, p. 4; "Aerial Looper of the LoopLady Victoria," *Cincinnati Enquirer*, February 24, 1914, p. 4; Maria Montessori (1870-1952) developed the Montessori method of education as a system for training and instructing young children. The fundamental aim of her system is self-education by the children themselves accompanied by special emphasis on the training of the senses; *The Random House Dictionary of the English Language*, rev. ed. (1973), s.v. "Montessori," p. 928.

18. Coligny, "Aerial Looper of the LoopLady Victoria," p. 4.

19. Coligny, "A Million Surplus Women," *Cincinnati Enquirer*, February 26, 1920, p. 4; Briol's statements are very similar to those of members of the American eugenics movement. For a discussion of eugenics see for example Kenneth M. Ludmerer, *Genetics and American Society: A Historical Appraisal*, (Baltimore, Maryland, 1972); Daniel Kevles, *In the Name of Eugenics: Genetics and the Uses of Human Heredity* (New York, 1985).

20. For a general discussion of trends in the area of women and family from 1900-1930 see Steven Mintz and Susan Kellogg, *Domestic Revolutions: A Social History of American Family Life* (New York, 1988), pp. 107-132.

21. Coligny, "A Veil Over Their Eyes," *Cincinnati Enquirer*, June 12, 1915, p. 6; "Learning to Be Blind—A Spiritual Miracle," *Cincinnati Enquirer*, December 29, 1915, p. 4; "The 'War Babies' Problem," *Cincinnati Enquirer*, May 14, 1915, p. 6.

22. Coligny, "Political Economic and Military Class in Russia, the Lack of Transport and the Threat of Famine," *Cincinnati Enquirer*, October 13, 1917, p. 6; "Send for Lloyd-George," *Cincinnati Enquirer*, June 17, 1916, p. 4; "A Universal or True Allied Language," *Cincinnati Enquirer*, May 12, 1917, p. 4; "Two Verdun Heroes Who Are Directing the Military Destiny of France," *Cincinnati Enquirer*, May 19, 1917, p. 4; "Foch, Our Chief and Types of French and German Generals," *Cincinnati Enquirer*, May 30, 1918.

23. Coligny, "The Massacre of Innocents," *Cincinnati Enquirer*, June 16, 1917, p. 4.

24. Coligny, "Invasion: French Women Speak," *Cincinnati Enquirer*, May 1, 1917; "Give Germany Justice—Nothing More," *Cincinnati Enquirer*, November 7, 1918, p. 6.

25. For a discussion of anti-German sentiment in the United States during and following World War I see Paul L. Murphy, *World War I and the Origin of Civil Liberties in the United States* (New York, 1970).

26. Coligny, "Summon Wilhelm Hohenzollern as a Fugitive From Justice," *Cincinnati Enquirer*, January 26, 1920, p. 6; "Summon on the All Highest Too," *Cincinnati Enquirer*, February 6, 1920, p. 6; "The War is Not Over," *Cincinnati Enquirer*, March 16, 1920, p. 6; "Anglo-Phobia," *Cincinnati Enquirer*, September 1, 1920, p. 6; "A German Gentleman Officer," *Cincinnati Enquirer*, March 6, 1920, p. 4.; "The Extermination of the

Romanoffs," *Cincinnati Enquirer*, September 25, 1920, p. 6.

27. Briol's close friends, Professor Kenneth Caster and Dorothy Muegel, and his nephew David T. Harvey, emphasized in interviews that Briol's hatred of Germans and Bolshevism was based on politics and not ethnic prejudice; K. Caster interview; D. Harvey interview; interview with Dorothy Muegel conducted at the home of Kenneth and Anne Caster in Cincinnati, July 24, 1989.

28. Coligny, "The Curse of Class Tyranny," *Cincinnati Enquirer*, March 4, 1920, p. 6; "Bolshevism vs. the Christian World," *Cincinnati Enquirer*, January 19, 1920, p. 6; "World Revolution," *Cincinnati Enquirer*, March 3, 1920, p. 6; "Crucifixions of Christianity," *Cincinnati Enquirer*, April 2, 1920.

29. For examples of Briol's "Red Scare" sentiments see Coligny, "As Others and We See Ourselves," *Cincinnati Enquirer*, February 26, 1920, p. 6; "The Old Enemy in Our Midst," *Cincinnati Enquirer*, March 2, 1920, p. 4.

30. To date I have not discovered who the Chinese scholar Briol met in New Orleans was.

31. Coligny, "Japanophobia," *Cincinnati Enquirer*, October 30, 1919, p. 6; "Japan and America," *Cincinnati Enquirer*, January 14, 1920, p. 4; "Beating Asian Drums of the Next War," *Cincinnati Enquirer*, January 20, 1920, p. 4; for an earlier discussion of Japan by Briol see "The Significance of the Mexican Envoy's Enthusiastic Reception in Japan," *Cincinnati Enquirer*, February 19, 1914, p. 4; "China," *Cincinnati Enquirer*, January 21, 1920.

32. It may also be significant that Briol's soon to be sister-in-law, Ruth Emerson Hannaford, was a missionary in Japan; telephone interview conducted with Jan Briol McLean, Paul and Mary Briol's daughter, August 21 and September 16, 1989.

33. Coligny, "Oliver Twist Home Closed," *Cincinnati Enquirer*, November 1, 1920, p. 6 was his final article. There is no reference to his leaving the paper in this or subsequent "Old-World Chit-chat" columns.

34. Interview conducted with Anne Caster at her home in Cincinnati July 24, 1989; K. Caster interview; J. McLean interview.

35. J. McLean interview; McLean has these letters in her possession.

36. J. McLean interview; Henderson, p. 2.

37. Miss E. Antoinette Ely's Clifton School for Young Ladies was well known as a private college preparatory school which trained female students "for admission into any of the colleges open to women." The school opened in 1896 and operated until 1920 when it closed suddenly without explanation; Geoffrey J. Giglierano and Deborah A. Overmyer with Frederic L. Propas, *The Bicentennial Guide to Greater Cincinnati: A Portrait of Two Hundred Years* (Cincinnati, 1988), p. 228.

38. The Ohio Military Institute was a private preparatory school for boys which was intended to provide "the influence of vigorous male control and example." Where, as the school's catalogue explained, boys needs for a "virile atmosphere of the military school," could be met. The school's last class graduated in 1958. The property was then sold to the Cincinnati Board of Education and reopened as Aiken High School; *Ibid.*, pp. 496-497.

39. J. Briol interview; D. Harvey interview.

40. A. Caster interview; D. Muegel interview.

41. No business records for The Book Shelf have been located to date, however, the 1930-1931 Cincinnati *City Directory* lists these individuals as members of the board: Robert A. Taft, president; Mrs. George Warrington, vice president; Carl Werner, secretary; Mrs. I.J. Cooper, treasurer; *City Directory*, 81 (Cincinnati, 1930), p. 279.

42. "Lovers of Literature Find Old Favorites at BookShelf's Opening," *Commercial Tribune*, May 10, 1921, p. 3.

43. K. Caster interview; A. Caster interview; J. Briol interview; Henderson, p. 2.

44. Briol, *The City of Rivers and Hills*.

45. The *Cincinnati Enquirer* reported that the company was approximately $23,000 in debt; "Receiver For Book Shelf," *Cincinnati Enquirer*, November 13, 1931, p. 15.

46. Robert Alphonso Taft (1889-1953) was the son of President and Supreme

Court Chief Justice William Howard Taft. His nickname, "Mr. Republican," aptly suggests his political ideals. Taft served as a U.S. Senator from 1938 until his death in 1953. He was considered a favorite for the Republican Presidential nomination in 1952, but lost to Dwight D. Eisenhower. A *Cincinnati Enquirer* article published acknowledging the centennial of Taft's birth described him as "an unwavering believer in sound fiscal policy, in balanced budgets and in controlling inflation, which he viewed as a mortally dangerous disease." Francis Lowenheim, "He Was 'Mr. Republican,'" *Cincinnati Enquirer*, September 10, 1989, pp. J:1, 5; see also James T. Patterson, *Mr. Republican: A Biography of Robert A. Taft* (Boston, 1972).

47. Jan Briol contends that her parents grieved for many years over the loss of their son. A. Caster describes the Briols as very happy at the birth of their daughter and noted that "Jan was the apple of Paul's eye." J. Briol and A. Caster interviews.

48. Frederick Way, Jr., *The Log of the Betsy Ann* (New York, 1933); Clark B. Firestone, *Sycamore Shores* (New York, 1936).

49. Briol's collection includes portraits of area families and individuals such as the Emersons, Frank Davis Gorman, Henry Goodyear, the Pease family, and many others; CHS Briol photographic collection.

50. A Caster interview; interview conducted with Benjamin Klein at his home in Cincinnati in August 3, 1989; Mr. Klein, co-founder of the Cincinnati printing and lithograph company Young and Klein, worked with Briol on a number of projects. He remembers that the time allocated to complete their work sessions was usually determined by the length of time it took to share a generous bottle of wine.

51. Some of these photographers are included in Cincinnati Historical Society, *Paul Briol: Cincinnati 1925-1950* (Cincinnati, 1981).

52. Mary Briol most likely worked on the Federal Writers' Project of the Works Progress Administration's (WPA) publication *Cincinnati: A Guide to the Queen City and Its Neighbors* (1943) which was the last volume produced in the WPA's American Guide Series. The Cincinnati Historical Society produced a reprint edition of the guide in 1987; Cincinnati Historical Society, *The WPA Guide to Cincinnati: Cincinnati, A Guide to the Queen City and Its Neighbors*, (Cincinnati, 1987); Mary Briol studied pre-school education at the University of Cincinnati when her daughter Jan was young. She recruited the eight students for her school from the surrounding College Hill neighborhood; J. Mclean interviews.

53. *Ibid.*

54. Foster, Ohio (also known as Foster's Crossing and Foster's, Ohio) is a tiny town originally settled by German immigrants along the banks of the Little Miami River. For many years a thriving flour mill operated on the river's bank. The town's picturesque location and access to the Dixie Highway encouraged its growth as a popular resort area. Hoppe's Island, complete with picnic grounds, refreshment stands, a beach, and dance pavilion drew visitors to the are. There were also a number of privately owned cottages, such as Briol's, located in the park's vicinity. The area remained a popular retreat until the 1950's. Construction of a 3-C highway viaduct in the 1930's literally directed traffic over Foster and eventually led to its decline as a resort. "Foster: Community Was Once a Landing on River when Little Miami Main Means of Transportation," *Lebanon Western Star*, June 30, 1976, p. 64; Tom McRoberts, "Remember Hoppe's Island?" *Middletown Banner*, August 20, 1980; "Morrow of Yesteryear," *Morrow Little Miami Express*, October 19, 1981, p. 2; Edwina Essex, "Dance Hall, Mill Make . . . .History at Foster," *Lebanon Western Star*, May 15, 1974, p. 8-A; Jim Myers, "Singular or Plural? Village Name 'Fosters' Confusion," *Dayton Daily News*, date unavailable, copy of article located at Warren County Historical Society (WCHS) in Lebanon, Ohio, Box 58; a run of the *Warren County Western Star* on microfilm is also available at WCHS; information on Shiro Tashiro was found in the *University of Cincinnati Annual and Catalogue* located at the University of Cincinnati Archives and Rare Books library in Blegen Library on campus.

55. Information about Briol's camp was gathered in interviews conducted with A. Caster, K. Caster, D. Harvey, J. McLean, D. Muegel. Curiously Briol appears to have taken few photographs of the Camp.

56. All interviewees agreed on their opinions of Mary Briol; A. Caster. K. Caster, D. Harvey, J. McLean, D. Muegel.

57. David T. Harvey (b. October 9, 1933) lived with the Briols' in their College Hill home from the time he was in fifth grade until he entered college. Harvey states that he is very appreciative of the opportunity the Briols' generosity. He acknowledges that most of his contacts with the Briols were with his "Aunt Mary" and his cousin Jan. In fact, although Harvey remembers "Uncle Paul" fondly, he says that their relationship was somewhat strained at times. This was especially true when Harvey failed to complete his chores and Briol would ask him, "Why do you eat?"; suggesting that he "should earn his keep;" D. Harvey interview.

58. Interviews conducted with A. Caster and D. Muegel.

59. Mary Briol, similar to other members of the Cincinnati Woman's City Club, was active in local Cincinnati Charter Party politics. Paul Briol was also a Charter Party supporter, but did not actively campaign for Party candidates. However, he is listed as a member of the Cincinnatus Association in a history of that group's work with the Charter Party; Louis Leonard Tucker, *Cincinnati's Citizen Crusaders: A History of the Cincinnatus Association, 1920-1965*, (Cincinnati, 1967), p. 242; for a more general history of the Charter Party and reform see Ralph A. Straetz, *PR Politics in Cincinnati: Thirty-two Years of City Government Through Proportional Representation* (New York, 1958); for a history of the Cincinnati Woman's City Club see Andrea Tuttle Kornbluh, *Lighting the Way: The Woman's City Club of Cincinnati, 1915-1965* (Cincinnati, 1986).

60. D. Harvey interview.

61. Cincinnati *City Directory*, 1939); the directory lists no downtown studio for Briol in its 1945 or 1946 volumes, however, the directory does show that Briol had a studio located on the fifth floor of 811 Race Street from 1947 through 1955. The Cincinnati *City Directory*, vols. 1939-1956.

62. J. McLean interview; copy of correspondence from Jan McLean to Jane Lotspeich March 6, 1963, in McLean's possession; *Look*, "Look at America: The Country You Know and Don't Know," (Boston, 1946).

63. *Ibid.*; A. Caster interview.

64. B. Klein interview; Owen Findsen, "Photos Make the City Beautiful," *Cincinnati Enquirer*, November 8, 1981, p. G:7.

65. J. McLean interview.

66. Briol's daughter Jan does not recall the incident in Covington, but a 1950 *Cincinnati Enquirer* article reported that it had occurred nine years earlier; "Photographer, 36 Others Hurt in Bus Crash," *Cincinnati Enquirer*, June 4, 1950, p. 1.

67. Mrs. Joselyn Farmer resided at 5700 Belmont Avenue in Cincinnati. She was thirty-nine years old at the time of the accident. Farmer received a Ph.D. in chemistry from the University of Cincinnati and worked as a chemist. Although she survived, she never really recovered from her injuries resulting from the crash.

68. "Photographer, 36 Others Hurt in Bus Crash," p. 1; "Briol Skidded On Wet Road; Report on Auto-Bus Crash," *Cincinnati Enquirer*, June 5, 1950, p. I:4; "35 Persons Injured in Bus-Auto Crash, Improving," *Lebanon Western Star*, June 8, 1950, pp. 1, 8.

69. Interviews conducted with A. Caster, K. Caster, D. Harvey, J. McLean, D. Muegel.

70. Janet "Jan" Briol McLean (b. 1923) graduated from the University of Cincinnati. She tried industrial design, but spent most of her working career as a psychiatric occupational therapist. While in Cincinnati she worked in the General Hospital's Psychiatric Department. McLean and her first husband, Frank Chinnock, an editor for *Readers Digest*, lived with their four children in Katonah, New York. After her parents' death, McLean remarried and currently lives with her husband in Connecticut. They also have a summer home in Gig Harbor, Washington. McLean remembers her father

24

encouraging her to become interested in photography, but she was not able to fully acquire the skill. She appears to be the only "student" Briol ever had.

71. Jane Lotspeich is a contemporary of Jan McLean; undated letter to Mrs. Robert Hestorff from Lotspeich, copy on possession of J. McLean.

72. Margaret Weaver, "Exhibit Focuses on Briol," *Cincinnati Post-Times Star*, April 22, 1963, p. 3.

73. "The Prints of Paul Briol," *Cincinnati Enquirer Pictorial Magazine*, May 5, 1963, pp. 30-35; "Briol Prints To Be Featured At Photography Exhibit," *Cincinnati Enquirer*, May 5, 1963, p. A-3.

74. "Mary Emerson Briol," *Cincinnati Enquirer*, February 16, 1968, p. 26.

75. "Paul Briol Rites Set, Photographic Artist," *Cincinnati Enquirer*, August 6, 1969, p. 14.

76. *Ibid.*; CHS, *Paul Briol: Cincinnati 1925-1050*, p. 1; Rosemary Munsen, "Sesquicentennial To Be A Celebration," *Cincinnati Enquirer*, October 7, 1981, p. C-3; Findsen, "Photos Make The City Beautiful," p. G-7.

77. Margaret Josten, "Vintage Cincinnati Is Looking good In UC's Briol Show," *Cincinnati Enquirer*, February 22, 1983, p. D-9.

78. "Pictures by Photography," copy of undated advertisement done by Walter F. Haehnle Agency for Paul Briol located in Briol files of the Historic New Orleans Collection, New Orleans, Louisiana.

Mary Briol possessed the spirit, intelligence, and elegance her husband found so attractive in women.

Paul Briol:
An Appreciation

Steven W. Plattner

The year 1989 marks the sesquicentennial of Louis Jacques Mande Daguerre's announcement of the Daguerreotype, the extraordinary invention which allowed one to fix a photographic image permanently on a copper plate and enabled humanity to freeze a moment in time.

For 150 years since Daguerre's revelation, Cincinnati has been both a home to, and a subject for, dozens of prominent photographers. In the midst of photography's sesquicentennial anniversary, it is especially fitting to honor and commemorate the one hundredth anniversary of the birth of Cincinnati photographer Paul Briol, the creator of an unmatched photographic record of the Queen City from the 1920's through the 1950's.

Rich as it is, Cincinnati's place in the history of photography has been somewhat neglected. As one of America's largest and fastest-growing inland cities at the time of Daguerre's announcement in January 1839, Cincinnati quickly established itself as a center for photography. In 1840 daguerreotypist Ezekiel Hawkins opened Cincinnati's first photograph gallery. By 1848 Charles Fontayne and William Southgate Porter created one of the best-known cityscapes of Daguerrian period, the eight-piece "whole plate" panorama of Cincinnati as viewed from Covington. During the 1840's and 1850's, daguerreotypes — nearly all of them portraits — were made in several downtown studios by a number of able daguerrian artists, including Thomas Faris and one of America's earliest black photographers, James P. Ball, proprietor of the lavish Ball's Daguerrian Gallery of the West located on Fourth Street.

With the invention of the albumen printing papers and the collodion wet plate negatives, photographers could make multiple prints of the same image, and perhaps more important, found it possible to take their cameras into the field and out of the studio. The daguerreotype quickly grew outmoded. Nevertheless, Cincinnati remained in the forefront of American cities with active photographic communities. Photographers like Leon Van Loo, H. Rohrer, Charles Waldack, James Landy, J.W. Winder, C.H. Muhrman, and J. Harry Hoover not only operated portrait studios, but also took their cameras into the streets,

photographing buildings, businesses, and prominent points of interest. Collectively, these photographers compiled a burgeoning record of Cincinnati, though only a minute body of their work has survived to the present day.

Photographic documentation continued to grow in Cincinnati at the beginning of the twentieth century. Cincinnati newspapers began to print photographic halftones near the turn of the century. In 1888 George Eastman's introduction of the Bullseye No. 1 camera allowed photographs to be taken by anyone who could afford the camera and the processing of flexible roll film and prints. While Eastman's innovation gave the average person the opportunity to record a visual image, it signaled a turn away from the technical mastery and sense of aesthetics formerly required of competent professional photographers.

As a photographic artist, Paul Briol was something of an anomaly among Cincinnati photographers. During the 1930's and 1940's, while most of his contemporaries turned to handheld 35 millimeter and 2-1/4 x 2-1/4 inch cameras, Briol devoted his fullest abilities to portraying Cincinnati, using an awkward wooden 8 x 10 inch view camera, perched atop a tripod. Aside from the fact that he used presensitized sheet film rather than having to coat his own glass plates as photographers did at the time of the Civil War, this choice of techniques could not have been more cumbersome or rigorous.

In the present age of Polaroid instant photography and 35 millimeter autofocus/autoexposure cameras, it is difficult, perhaps even impossible, to comprehend fully the care and forethought that characterize the work of Paul Briol. Working under such technical and physical constraints required a special sort of discipline and demanded a deeper way of seeing from him. As is evident in his work, Briol contemplated the scenes before him, choosing his lens, his exposure, and his composition with the utmost care. He combed the city, seeking out vantage points, sensing moods — ultimately finding and sharing great beauty with those of us incapable of seeing and recording it on our own.

Paul Briol was particularly capable of infusing his prints with drama. In the darkroom, Briol was a master of merging two images into a single print. In the Paul Briol Collection at The Cincinnati Historical Society, there are a number of negatives of clouds, which Briol ably printed above

Steven W. Plattner, author of
Roy Stryker: U.S.A. 1943-1950, has an M.A. in history from George Washington University.

skylines to add power and expression to his photographic images.

While much of Briol's best-known work depicted the beauty of Cincinnati's rivers and hills — steamboats and stevedores on the Ohio River, views of Mt. Adams and the smokey haze over downtown, and the magic of Coney Island, to name just three, Briol made a living for himself and his family through photography. Not surprisingly, the majority of 8 x 10 inch negatives in his collection consists of assignments documenting a wide range of Cincinnati institutions, including the *Cincinnati Times-Star*, Union Terminal, Lunken Airport, Baldwin Piano Company, the University of Cincinnati, various hospitals and charitable organizations, and portraits of affluent Cincinnatians.

Paul Briol could transform a mundane assignment — like documenting buildings and facilities at the University of Cincinnati — into a challenge to create beauty. One example is his photograph of a lab in the University's Physics Department, a beautifully composed image which, intentionally or not, immediately brings to mind the work of the Constructivist painter Kandinsky.

Though he disdained much of the portraiture he did of various Cincinnatians, many of the images which resulted from such assignments reveal a great deal about their subjects, and at times, about Briol and his incisive eye. There are wonderful portraits of a black maid and chauffeur employed by one wealthy family. In another portrait, members of the Pease family appear remote and aloof. While in another portrait an older black couple seems far more comfortable and oblivious to Briol and his camera. Finally, Briol demonstrates his sensitivity for the grief of an elderly woman who has lost a grandson in World War II.

Whether photographing passenger trains leaving Union Terminal, a Reds game at Crosley Field, or pigeons perched on the outstretched arms of the Genius of Waters atop the Tyler Davidson Fountain, the more than 6,000 extant images made by Paul Briol constitute an unequaled photographic record of Cincinnati during the twentieth century.

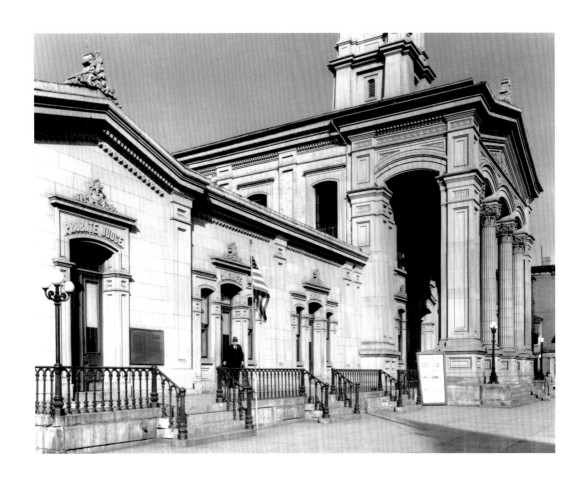

Chronology

1888
June 6. Paul Briol's parents, Fannie Nusbaum and Pierre Phillippe Briol were married in Greenbay, Wisconsin. A native of Villy, Switzerland, Pierre Briol was ordained into the Presbyterian ministry in San Francisco in 1887.

1889
September 18. Paul Auguste Briol was born in Spencer, Massachusetts.

1893
June 22. Almee Fannie Virginia Briol, Paul's only sibling, was born in Carthage, Missouri.

1903
The Briol family moved to New Orleans where Pierre Briol founded the First French Presbyterian Church of New Orleans in 1905.

1908
Paul Briol graduated from high school and moved to St. Louis, lived with his uncle, Charles Nusbaum, and worked for a local newspaper.

1909
Briol moved to Cincinnati and lived with the Reverend Louis G. Hoeck, pastor of the Church of the New Jerusalem (Swedenborgian) at 825 Oak Street. He joined the staff of the Cincinnati *Commercial Tribune* as a journalist and photographer. November 26. The *Tribune* published Briol's first professionally credited work titled "Leopold Stokovski [sic] and New Symphony Orchestra of which he has recently become the director."

1910
Briol left the *Commercial Tribune* to join the staff of the *Cincinnati Enquirer*.

1912
May 28. He authored the first "Old-World Chitchat" column for the *Enquirer* under the pseudonym, M. Coligny. The columns ran regularly Monday-Saturday through November 1, 1920.

1915
Paul Briol met Mary Elizabeth Emerson at Grace Episcopal Church in College Hill, a Cincinnati suburb. Mary Emerson, daughter of Mary Adelpha Simpson and Dudley Emerson, was born in 1884 and grew up in College Hill.

1920
Briol left the *Cincinnati Enquirer* to become the manager of The Book Shelf.

May 26. He married Mary Elizabeth Emerson and resided at the north east corner of Belmont and Larch avenues in College Hill.

1921
May 9. The Book Shelf opened its doors at 112 Garfield Place, the former home of the Seasongood family.

1923
Daughter Joan (Jan) Briol was born August 4.

1925
Briol authored *City of Rivers and Hills*. Published by The Book Shelf, this collection of black and white images was dedicated to his wife Mary.

1930
Forced into bankruptcy by the Depression, The Book Shelf was closed.

1932
Briol opened a photographic studio and by 1932 was located in the Doctors' Building, 19 Garfield Place.

1933
The studio moved to the eighth floor of the Doctors' Building. Twenty-seven photographs were published in *The Log of the Betsy Ann* by Captain Frederick Way, Jr. (New York: McBride).

mid-1930's
Briol bought a Japanese style cottage from Dr. Shiro Tashiro, professor of biochemistry at the University of Cincinnati Medical School, 1919-1955. The "camp" was on a steep bank of the Little Miami River in Foster, Ohio.

1936
Twenty-two photographs were published in *Sycamore Shores* by Clark B. Firestone (New York: McBride).

1937
Spring. Mary and Jan went to Japan to visit Mary's sister and brother-in-law, Ruth and Howard Hannaford. After three months in Japan, they visited China, crossed the Soviet Union on the TransSiberian Railroad, stopped in Moscow, continued through Poland, Hungary, and much of Europe.

1938
Briol moved his office to 114 Garfield Place.

1946
Photographs by Briol were included in *Look at America: The Country You Know and Don't Know* by the editors of *Look* magazine (Boston: Houghton Mifflin). Accompanied by friends, Briol traveled west in his 1939 Hudson, visiting Yosemite, California, and photographing the country.

1947
The studio was moved to the space it occupied until 1955 on the fifth floor at 811 Race Street.

1950
June 3. Briol was severely injured when his car skidded during a rain storm and collided with a Greyhound bus on Route 42 about one mile south of Mason, Ohio.

1955
No longer able to carry on his business, Briol closed the downtown studio. His negatives and prints were moved to the carriage house at his home at 1812 Larch Avenue, College Hill.

1962
The Briols moved to Katonah, New York to live with their daughter. Over 6,000 negatives were given to The Cincinnati Historical Society.

1963
May 12-26. Through the efforts of his daughter and Jane Lotspeich and with the sponsorship of The Professional Photographers' Association of Greater Cincinnati, 300 prints from Briol's personal collection were shown at the "Paul Briol Exhibit" at the University of Cincinnati Student Union.

1968
February 16. Mary Elizabeth Emerson Briol died in Katonah, New York. Burial followed a memorial service at Spring Grove Cemetery in Cincinnati, February 20.

1969
August 3. Paul Auguste Briol died in a nursing home near his daughter's home in Katonah, New York. The memorial service and burial were at Spring Grove Cemetery, August 9.

1981
Paul Briol: Cincinnati 1925-1950, an appointment calendar with a selection of his photographs was published by The Cincinnati Historical Society.

1983
February 7-26. An exhibition, "Paul Briol Photographs: Cincinnati Focus 1925-1950," was held at the University of Cincinnati's Tangeman Center.

Paul Briol Negatives and Contact Prints at The Cincinnati Historical Society

When the Society received the Briol Collection in 1962, it was not in order and many images were neither labeled nor dated. The Society's curators grouped the images by topic and attempted to identify people and places using available resources. We did not find information about each image and we apologize for these omissions and the inaccuracies that certainly must be present.

A wooden-framed rollercoaster at Coney Island

Kahn's meat packing plant

Subject	Number of Prints
Amusements	
Coney Island	49
Moonlight Gardens	52
Sunlite Pool	12
Associations	
Association for the Blind	17
YMCA	4
YMCA (Camp Lenmary)	1
Banks	
Central Trust	66
First National	33
Bridges/Viaducts	
Central	1
Columbia Viaduct	18
Covered (Mt. Healthy)	2
Ida Street	6
McMillan Street	1
Western Hills	4
Buildings	
Carew Tower	7
Chamber of Commerce	1
City Hall	1
Music Hall	17
Business & Industry	
A & C Motor Sales	19
AMSCO Products Co.	2
American Book Co.	21
M.L. Andrew Co.	1
Argus Industries Inc.	12
Baldwin Piano Co.	9
Berghausen Chemical Co.	2
Beau Brummel Ties Inc.	1
Bruckmann Co. Brewers	5
Philip Carey & Co.	7
Carlton Machine Tool Co.	4
Chase Brass & Copper Co. Inc.	1
Cincinnati Bell Telephone	2
Cincinnati Gas & Electric Co.	21
Cincinnati Times-Star Co.	142
Clermont Hill Dairy	4
Coca-Cola Bottling Works Co.	78
Daly & Luehrman Carpet Co.	6
Diamond Alkali Co.	14
Fasfoto Finishing Service	2
Fostoria	25

Gardner-Richardson Co.	37
General Electric Co.	17
General Machinery Co.	37
Gruen Watch Co.	6
Heekin Can Co.	1
Kahn's Sons Co.	20
Kinnear Mfg. Co.	5
Wm. Koehl Co.	3
F.H. Lawson Co.	1
Ohio National Life Insurance Co.	7
Pease Woodwork Co. Inc.	18
Ponds (Burroughs Laboratories)	51
Rookwood Pottery	4
Rosebrook Clinical Laboratory	7
St. Joseph Paper Co.	3
Seagram Distillers Corp.	33
Strietmann Biscuit Co.	12
Tomlin Strause Welding	6
Wright Aeronautical Corp.	22
Unidentified	24
Cemeteries and Crematoriums	
Cincinnati Cremation Co.	
(Cincinnati Crematory)	26
Spring Grove Cemetery	20
Charitable Institutions	
Babies Milk Fund Association	26
Children's Convalescent Home	35
Children's Home	54
Clovernook Home and School for the Blind	32
Fresh Air Farm	11
Nursing Homes	10
Other	8
Churches	
Baptist	
Free Will Baptist Church	2
Ninth Street Baptist Church	14
Church of Christ	
Salem United Church of Christ	1
Episcopal	
Chapel of the Transfiguration	31
Christ Church	179
Christ Church (Glendale)	36
Grace Episcopal Church (College Hill)	3
St. Paul's Wayside Cathedral	6
Jewish (Hebrew)	
Isaac M. Wise Temple	11
Presbyterian	
College Hill Presbyterian Church	1
First Presbyterian Church of Glendale	9
Roman Catholic	
Church of the Immaculate Conception	6
St. Elizabeth (Church of Norwood)	53
Sts. Peter & Paul Church	11
St. Peter in Chains Cathedral	10
St. Xavier Church	9
Swedenborgian	
The Church of the New Jerusalem	11
Unitarian (Montgomery)	1
Unidentified	4

Health clinic sponsored by Babies Milk Fund

Hollyhocks, clouds, and a weathered fence

"The Pines," John Kilgour's home

The Public Library bookmobile of the 1940's

Court Street Market

Young harpist

Lytle Park band-
stand dedicated to
Mike Mullen

Ice scene on the
Ohio River

Hillsdale School
— Lotspeich
School in
Madisonville

Oscar Silverstein
shoe repair on
Vine Street

Mariemont, a
planned commu-
nity, opened in
1924

Cincinnati
streamlined elec-
tric streetcar

Bridge at Foster, Ohio

The University of Florida

Capitol building in Richmond, Virginia

Landscape from western trip

An artisan carving a marionette

Portfolio Photographs

Special thanks to Mark Eberhard, Eberhard & Eberhard, and Steven W. Plattner, The Hennegan Company, for selecting the photographs in the portfolio; to Pat Brand, Jr., Brand Studios, for processing the prints from the Briol negatives; to Cincinnati Historical Society staff: Linda J. Bailey, Photograph Librarian, and Laura L. Chace, The Frederick A. Hauck Librarian, for selecting photographs and compiling the catalogue to the negative and contact print collection.